Let's Go camping!

Written by Jillian Powell

Contents

☀ Collins

Worldwide camping

Camping gives you freedom to stay in a lot of different places – by the seaside, on a mountain, by a lake or in a forest. People go camping all over the world.

The highest campsite in the world at 8,300 metres is on Mount Everest, in Tibet.

Campsites with amazing views

Lamar Valley
Yellowstone National
Park, Wyoming, USA

Longitude 131°
campsite with views
of Uluru (Ayers Rock),
Australia

Ecocamp Patagonia
in the Torres del Paine
National Park, Chile

The Warren, Kent,
on top of England's
White Cliffs of Dover

Tent types

Four-season tents are strong enough to be used in cold temperatures on high mountains.

Lightweight summer tents are suitable for short, fair-weather trips.

Tents also come in different shapes and sizes, from small, light, backpacker tents, to family tents that can sleep four or more.

Dome tents are stable and good in snowy weather.

A-frame tents are light to carry but have less headroom.

Cabin tents are roomy and good for families.

Hoop tents are good in rain and snow.

5

Camping equipment

If you're camping somewhere away from the shops, you need to think ahead and pack carefully.

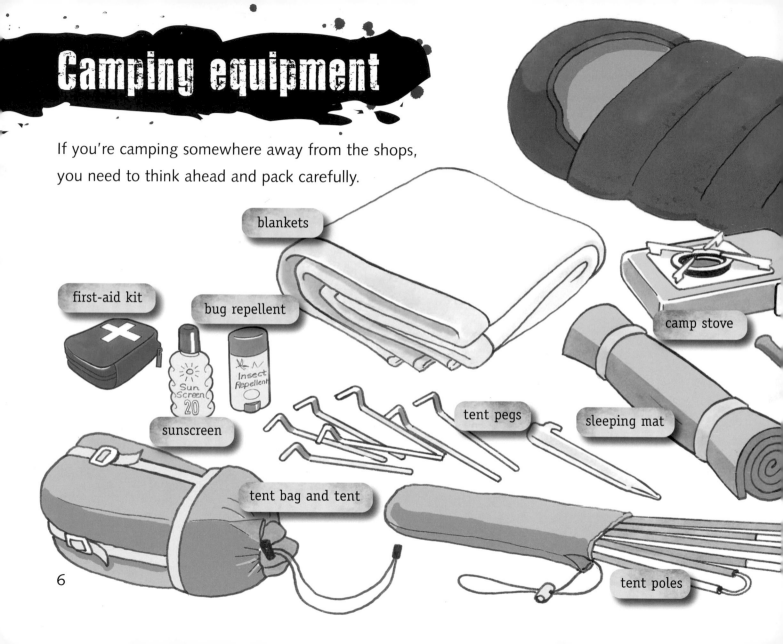

blankets

first-aid kit

bug repellent

camp stove

sunscreen

tent pegs

sleeping mat

tent bag and tent

tent poles

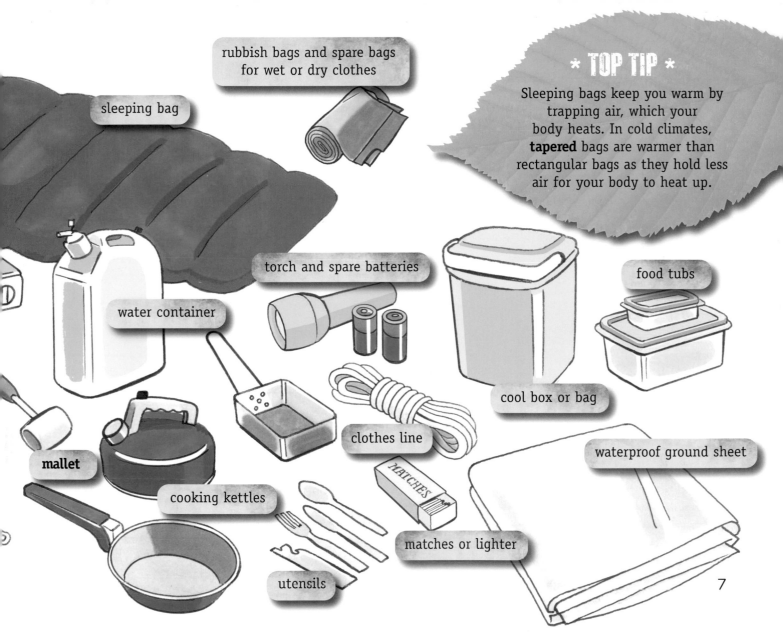

sleeping bag

rubbish bags and spare bags for wet or dry clothes

water container

torch and spare batteries

food tubs

cool box or bag

clothes line

mallet

waterproof ground sheet

cooking kettles

MATCHES

matches or lighter

utensils

7

The campsite

Choosing your campsite

There are lots of things to think about when you choose where to go camping. Reading a map can help you find a suitable place to camp.

🚐 ⛺ You can locate camping and caravan sites.

The map shows you features of the landscape such as woods, cliffs or marshy land. Camping too close to cliffs could be dangerous and you should avoid marshy land, which can flood.

The map shows you whether the land is flat or hilly. You'll need level ground to camp on. Look for **contour lines** that are wide apart.

When you're camping out in the countryside, you need to get permission from landowners. Maps show you the boundaries of forestry land, National Parks and private parks.

9

Campers need clean water nearby. Try to set up camp within a short walk from water, but don't camp too close to rivers or streams in case they burst their banks. Water can also attract biting insects like gnats and mosquitoes in summer.

Campers need water for drinking, washing and cooking.

Use the map to find footpaths, cycle trails and local attractions.

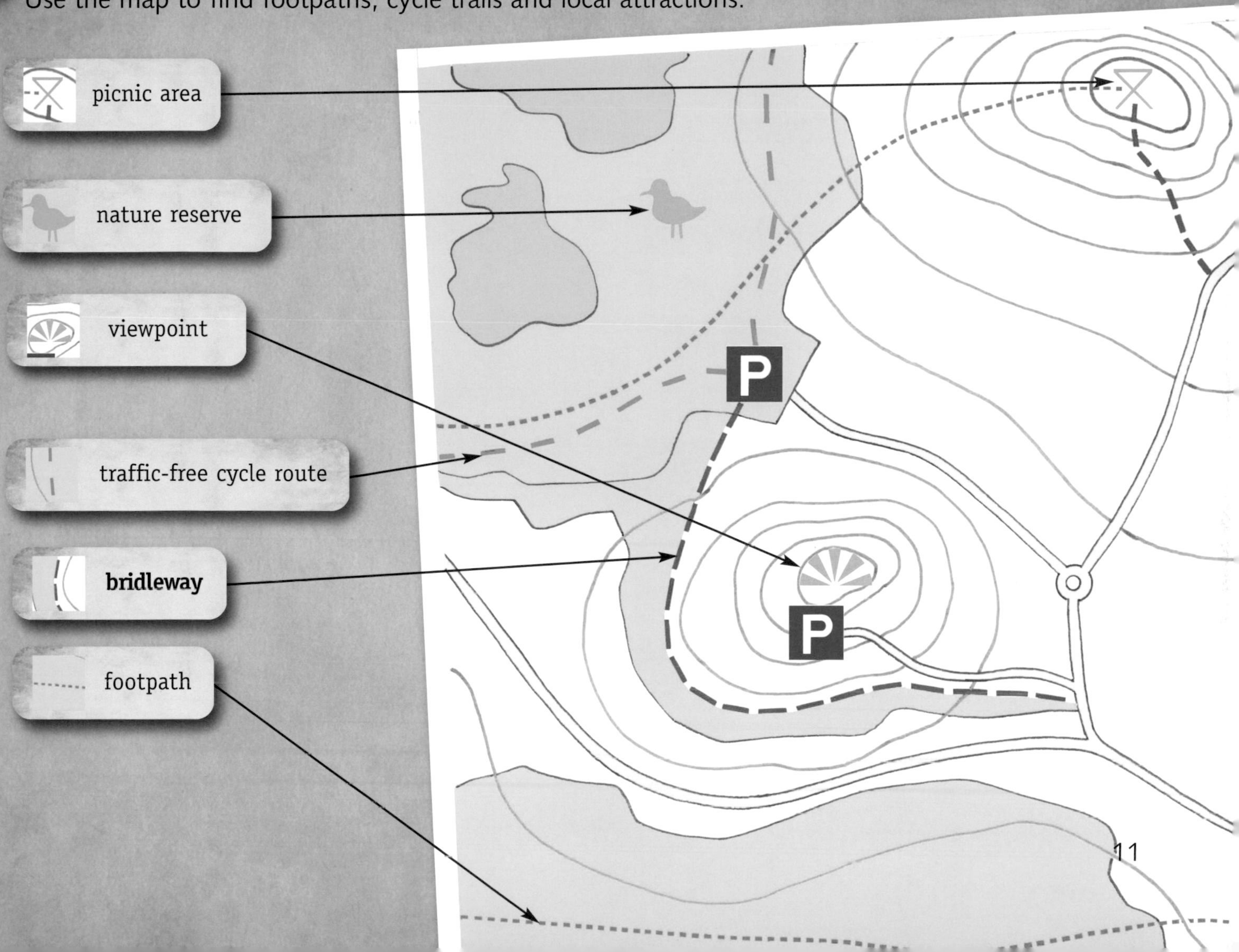

picnic area

nature reserve

viewpoint

traffic-free cycle route

bridleway

footpath

Setting up camp

When you've chosen your campsite, follow these tips for a comfortable camp.

Choose a level, shady and sheltered site. Don't pitch your tent in the middle of a field where people or animals could pass through.

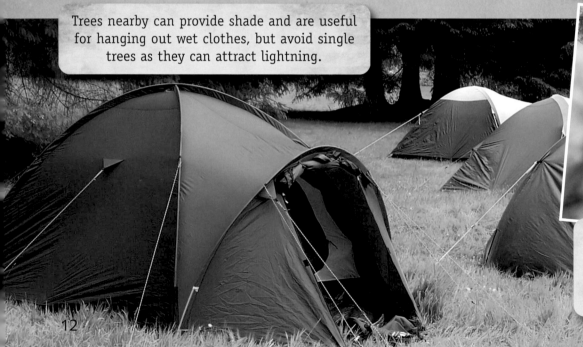

Do a finger test to check wind direction. This can help to prevent rain or smoke from a campfire blowing into your tent. Wet your finger and hold it up into the wind. You can tell the direction from which the wind is blowing by the side of your finger which feels coolest as the water **evaporates**.

Trees nearby can provide shade and are useful for hanging out wet clothes, but avoid single trees as they can attract lightning.

Check above you for danger from insect nests, or falling rocks or branches.

12

Avoid low ground, like valley bottoms. Warm air rises and cold air sinks so they can hold damp mist, cold air or frost. Low ground can also flood during heavy rain or if rivers burst their banks.

Pitch your tent where it won't damage long grass or wild flowers. Avoid stones, tree roots and ants' nests. Check for animal tracks, especially where animals may be going to find water.

Look to see where the sun is in the sky. Do you want to be in the shade, or wake up to see the sunrise? In a hot climate you may welcome shade, but in a cold climate, you may want the warmth of the sun.

The sun can help to warm a tent if you're camping somewhere cold.

Tools and skills

Pitching your tent

If you're camping, you'll need to learn how to pitch a tent.

Step-by-step guide

1 Unfold and connect the tent poles, then lay them out.

2 Insert the poles through the outer tent using the sleeves.

3 Erect and peg out the tent. Pull it taut.

* TOP TIP *

Loosen the guy lines at night and when rain is expected, as when rain or morning dew dries the guy lines will shrink and tighten.

4 Clip the inner tent to the inside, then peg in the **guy lines** if your tent has them.

15

Campfire cooking

There are different ways to cook outdoors. You can use a camping stove or a barbecue. Camping stoves use bottled gas as fuel.

You can heat water and food in a pan or a kettle. A Kelly Kettle is a special type of kettle that you fill with water, which is then heated to boiling point by lighting a fire inside it using twigs inside the double wall of the Kettle.

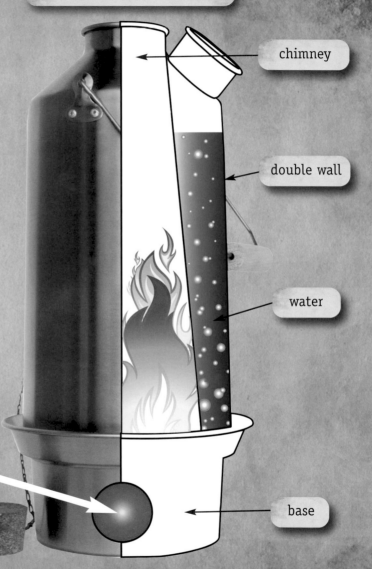

cross-section of a Kelly Kettle

chimney

double wall

water

base

fuel (twigs, moss, tree bark, pine cones)

16

Always store food off the ground away from pests and insects. Use waterproof containers and bags to keep food dry. Dehydrated and **freeze-dried foods** are high-energy foods that can be easily stored and carried. They cook in a pouch or pan when boiling water is added.

freeze-dried food packets

17

Exploring your surroundings

Reading locations

When you're camping, you can use a map and **compass** to find the direction of your campsite and to explore your surroundings.

Use a compass to find north, south, east and west. Hold it out flat in your hand so that the needle can turn freely. The red arrow always points to the north.

There are also ways to find out where you are without a compass. The sun rises in the east and sets in the west, so at midday the sun is roughly in the south.

An hour or more before or after midday, you can use a shadow stick to check your direction. Plant a straight stick about 0.5 metres long into bare ground. Mark where the end of its shadow falls with a pebble. Wait for 20 minutes, then mark the end of the new shadow with another pebble. Draw a straight line between the two markers. This marks east to west. Draw a line through it to mark north and south.

Tracking signs

If you're camping in a group and decide to go walking or cycling, it can be useful to learn some tracking signs so that if part of the group gets behind, they can follow the leaders. Trackers use simple signs made from stones, twigs or leaves.

this way

no entry or danger

turn left or turn right

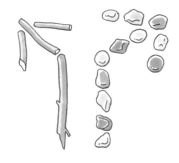

water ahead

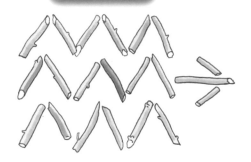

obstacle ahead

split group – two went left, four went right

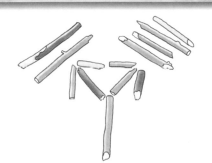

gone home

21

Animal tracking

Living outdoors brings you into close contact with wildlife. As well as spotting birds and animals, you can learn how to track them from their footprints and other clues. You can go tracking after snow or heavy rain, or in muddy soil near river banks.

* TOP TIP *

Find out what kind of animals live in the area before you go tracking.

Near water, look for the tracks of animals like otters, or water birds like ducks and **coots**.

otter print

coot print

Rabbits and hares land with their larger hind feet ahead of their front feet.

rabbit print: hind foot and front foot

Claws appear as triangular marks at the front of the print. Cats keep their claws in when they walk or run, but dogs and foxes show claw marks.

cat print

fox print

Two-toe tracks are usually deer.

deer print

Four toes on the front feet and five on the hind feet may be a **rodent** like a **vole** or a squirrel.

squirrel print: front foot and hind foot

Five toes on the front feet and five on the hind feet may be a badger, otter or mink.

badger print

As well as tracking animal footprints, look out for other signs of animal life such as burrows, gnawed leaves, droppings or pellets.

Birds including owls and kingfishers produce pellet waste from their beaks. Owl pellets can sometimes be found under trees or fence posts where they have landed.

Badgers live in underground setts in woodland.

Deer droppings are oval-shaped.

owl pellets

23

Flora and fauna

While you're out and about, look out for natural objects like leaves or pine cones in an evergreen forest, feathers dropped by birds, or shells at the seaside. But remember not to pick wild flowers or interfere with birds' eggs.

You can look for edible berries like damsons, **sloes** or blackberries, and plants like wild garlic and stinging nettles, which you can make into nettle soup.

bird's feather and
pine cones

Never eat any berries, plants or **fungi** that you're not sure about as they may be poisonous and could make you ill. Always check with a grown-up who knows about them first.

Death cap mushrooms are often found under oak trees and are deadly poisonous.

damsons

death cap mushroom

After dark, listen for sounds like the call of owls, deer or foxes. You might spot **nocturnal** animals like bats or badgers.

Look for bats silhouetted against an open sky.

* TOP TIP *

You can make a simple moth trap by hanging up a white sheet as it gets dark. Use a torch to light up the sheet to attract moths and try to count the different species you see in one night. You can also try painting a mixture of sugar and water on to a wall or post to attract moths or daytime butterflies.

Looking after the countryside

Remember to follow the countryside code when you're camping.

Always close gates after you and take extra care when there are animals in the fields. A gate left open could let animals stray on to roads. Keep dogs on leads when you're walking through fields of sheep or cattle, especially when they have young.

Please keep dogs under close control

Remember that noise, especially at night-time, can disturb wildlife as well as people living nearby.

Never leave litter behind. Cans, glass bottles and plastic bags can all harm wildlife.

When your camping trip is over, leave the campsite as tidy as you found it, or tidier!

* TOP TIP *
When you're washing clothes or dishes, use an **eco-friendly** no-rinse soap.

Glossary

bridleway   a path to ride or walk horses on

compass   an instrument which has a magnetised needle and is used for finding directions

contour lines   wavy lines on a map that show hills

coots   water birds with mainly black feathers

eco-friendly   causing as little damage as possible to the environment

evaporates   changes from a liquid to a vapour

freeze-dried foods   food that is preserved by being frozen quickly, then dried in a vacuum

fungi   things like mushrooms, toadstools and mould

guy lines   ropes that hold a tent in place

mallet   a type of hammer with a very large head that is flat at both ends

nocturnal   being active at night instead of during the day

purify   remove all germs and dirt

rodent   animals that have long teeth for chewing

sloes   small, blue-black blackthorn fruit

tapered   becoming narrower towards one end

vole   a small mouse-like creature

Index

Camping dos and dont's

DO

* think ahead and make sure you pack everything you need if you're away from shops.
* choose a level, shady site on which to pitch your tent.
* pitch your tent where it won't damage long grass or flowers.
* make sure there is a source of water to hand.
* check the wind direction before lighting a campfire.
* use an eco-friendly soap for washing dishes and clothes.
* always follow the countryside code.
* always carry a map, compass and safety equipment.
* always close gates after you.
* keep dogs on a lead.
* keep noise to a minimum.

Please keep dogs under close control

DON'T

* leave litter behind.
* pitch your tent in a field where there are animals.
* pitch your tent on low ground, such as a valley bottom, as it may be damp and even become flooded.
* pitch your tent near a single tree, as this could attract lightning.
* pitch your tent on stones, ants' nests or tree roots.
* pick wildflowers or interfere with birds' nests and eggs.
* eat wild berries, plants and fungi without checking first with an adult.
* leave food on the ground or it may attract pests and insects.

31

Ideas for guided reading

Learning objectives: recognise a range of suffixes, understanding how they modify meaning; develop and use specific vocabulary in different contexts; identify and make notes of the main points of sections of text; identify features that writers use; use layout, format, graphics and illustrations for different purposes

Curriculum links: Geography: Investigating our local area

Interest words: contour lines, mallet, tapered, purify, bridleway, evaporates, guy lines, compass, freeze-dried food, coots, vole, sloes, fungi, nocturnal, eco-friendly

Resources: whiteboard, writing materials, straight sticks, small pebbles

Getting started

This book can be read over two or more guided reading sessions.

- Read the blurb together and ask children whether any of them have been camping before, and what they already know about camping. Write their ideas on the whiteboard.

- Point out that this is an information book and discuss the features of these, e.g. contents, index, glossary.

Reading and responding

- Using the contents page, give each pair a section of text to read and make notes from, making sure all of the book is covered.

- Remind children to use the glossary for unfamiliar words and not to copy directly from the text, but to summarise in bullet points.

- Ask pairs to practise explaining information to each other, using pictures and diagrams in the text to help.

- Ask children to present the information they have learnt to the rest of the group, encouraging the group to ask questions and discuss the information.